SPEED ZONE

SUPERFAST MOTORCYCLES

by Alicia Z. Klepeis

pogo

Ideas for Parents and Teachers

Pogo Books let children practice reading informational text while introducing them to nonfiction features such as headings, labels, sidebars, maps, and diagrams, as well as a table of contents, glossary, and index.

Carefully leveled text with a strong photo match offers early fluent readers the support they need to succeed.

Before Reading

- "Walk" through the book and point out the various nonfiction features. Ask the student what purpose each feature serves.
- Look at the glossary together. Read and discuss the words.

Read the Book

- Have the child read the book independently.
- Invite him or her to list questions that arise from reading.

After Reading

- Discuss the child's questions. Talk about how he or she might find answers to those questions.
- Prompt the child to think more. Ask: Why can some motorcycles go so fast? Can you think of any other superfast vehicles?

Pogo Books are published by Jump!
5357 Penn Avenue South
Minneapolis, MN 55419
www.jumplibrary.com

Library of Congress Cataloging-in-Publication Data

Names: Klepeis, Alicia, 1971- author.
Title: Superfast motorcycles / by Alicia Z. Klepeis.
Description: Minneapolis, MN: Jump!, Inc., [2022]
Series: Speed zone
Includes index. | Audience: Ages 7-10
Identifiers: LCCN 2020050903 (print)
LCCN 2020050904 (ebook)
ISBN 9781645279648 (hardcover)
ISBN 9781645279655 (paperback)
ISBN 9781645279662 (ebook)
Subjects: LCSH: Motorcycles, Racing—Juvenile literature.
Classification: LCC TL442 .K59 2022 (print)
LCC TL442 (ebook) | DDC 629.227/5–dc23
LC record available at https://lccn.loc.gov/2020050903
LC ebook record available at https://lccn.loc.gov/2020050904

Editor: Eliza Leahy
Designer: Molly Ballanger

Photo Credits: Toa55/Shutterstock, cover; David Shao/Shutterstock, 1; Dragcam/Dreamstime, 3; Pavel L Photo and Video/Shutterstock, 4; Corinna Huter/Shutterstock, 5; Ivan Garcia/Shutterstock, 6-7; Tony Watson/Alamy, 8-9; otomobil/Shutterstock, 10; WENN Rights Ltd/Alamy, 11; AP Images, 12-13; Heritage Images/Getty, 14; Mau47/Shutterstock, 15; Hafiz Johari/Shutterstock, 16-17; Khunasoix/Dreamstime, 18-19; Michele Morrone/Shutterstock, 20-21; JULIE LUCHT/Shutterstock, 23.

Printed in the United States of America at Corporate Graphics in North Mankato, Minnesota.

TABLE OF CONTENTS

CHAPTER 1

READY TO RACE

A motorcycle race is about to start. Riders line up. They start their **engines**.

The race begins! The motorcycles screech off the starting line. Some go 250 miles (402 kilometers) per hour! That is more than four times faster than a car on the highway. They zip around the first corner. Vroom!

Superfast motorcycles compete in the MotoGP World Championship. These motorcycles are built for racing only. They are not available for the public to buy.

DID YOU KNOW?

The Daytona 200 is another famous race. It is held each spring in Daytona Beach, Florida. Riders drive 57 laps around a paved course.

Drag racing is another kind of motorcycle race. Two bikers race along a straight track that is a quarter mile (0.4 km) long. The speed record for this race is 264 miles (425 km) per hour.

A motorcycle needs a lot of **horsepower** (HP) to go this fast. This **force** is produced by the engine. HP also helps it **accelerate** quickly.

DID YOU KNOW?

The Kawasaki Ninja H2 has 310 HP. Count to five. In that time, the Ninja H2 can go from 0 to 100 miles (161 km) per hour!

drag race

CHAPTER 2

BRING THE POWER!

A motorcycle engine burns fuel in **cylinders**. A motorcycle with more cylinders burns fuel faster. Fast motorcycles usually have four cylinders. Some have as many as six!

engine

A supercharger makes a motorcycle even faster. How? It forces more air into the cylinders. This burns fuel faster. The engine produces more power.

Voxan
Wattman

Most superfast motorcycles run on gas. But some run on **electric power**. The Voxan Wattman is one. It has a top speed of 231 miles (372 km) per hour.

CHAPTER 3

SPEEDY DESIGN

Frame design can help a motorcycle go faster. **Fairings** are panels that attach to a bike's frame.

Fairings make a frame more **aerodynamic**. They cut down on **drag** when the bike changes direction.

winglet
agv
FIAMM
PRAMAC
43
indra
minsait
Lifter
PRAMAC
DUCATI

At high speeds, a bike is less **stable**. Why? **Wind pressure** increases. It can make the front wheel lift off the ground. **Winglets** give the bike better grip. Air flows over the winglets, pressing the bike toward the ground. This is called **downforce**.

Motorcycle tires are different from car tires. How? They are more curved on the sides. This shape helps a bike lean and turn corners.

TAKE A LOOK!

What are the parts of a superfast motorcycle? Take a look!

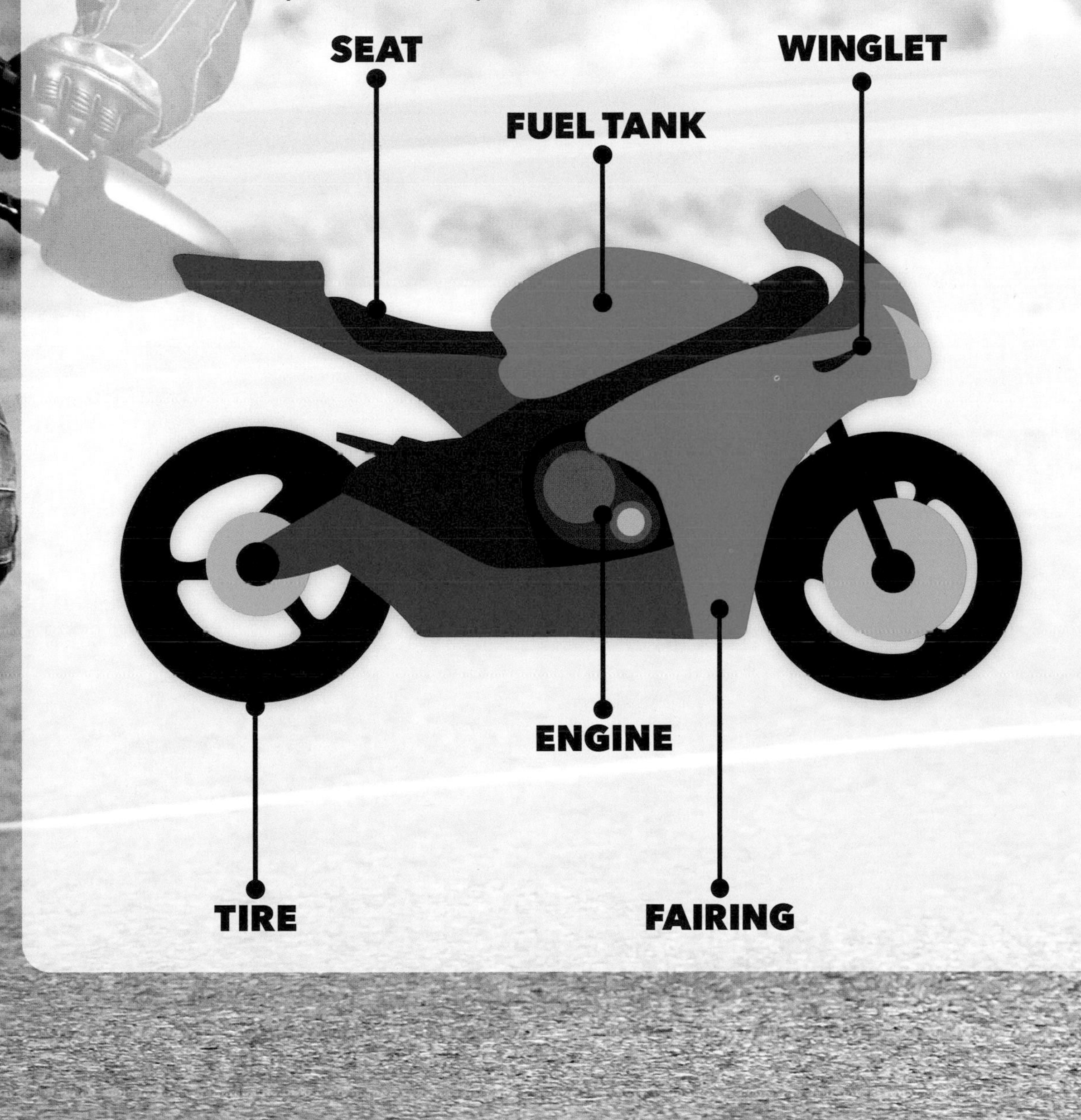

Fast motorcycles are made of strong but light materials. Why? It takes less power to speed up or slow down bikes that weigh less.

Engineers work to create speedier motorcycles. How fast do you think they will go in the future?

DID YOU KNOW?

Companies are working on motorcycles that can balance themselves. Imagine racing along with no fear of tipping over!

HONDA
MOTUL
HONDA

ACTIVITIES & TOOLS

TRY THIS!

BUILD YOUR OWN MOTORCYCLE

Design a motorcycle and see how fast it can go!

What You Need:

- pen or pencil
- paper
- various recycled materials (cardboard, bottles, etc.)
- scissors
- glue or tape
- coins or tiny weights

1. **Sketch a motorcycle design that you can make and that you think can move fast.**
2. **Look around your home for materials that you might be able to use to make your motorcycle. Pipe cleaners are easy to bend for a bike frame or handlebars. Plastic caps or modeling clay might make good wheels.**
3. **Use the materials you find to build the motorcycle you sketched.**
4. **When your motorcycle is ready, place it on the floor. Give it a push. How fast does it go? What if you add some coins or other weights? How does that affect the motorcycle's speed and distance? Why do you think that is?**

GLOSSARY

accelerate: To move faster and faster.

aerodynamic: Designed to move through the air easily and quickly.

cylinders: Enclosed spaces in engines where fuel is burned.

downforce: A downward aerodynamic force.

drag: The force that slows motion, action, or advancement.

electric power: Power supplied by or having to do with electricity.

engineers: People who are specially trained to design and build machines or large structures.

engines: Machines that make things move by using gasoline, steam, or another energy source.

fairings: Metal or plastic structures added to motorcycle frames to reduce drag.

force: Any action that produces, stops, or changes the shape or movement of an object.

frame: A basic structure that provides support for a vehicle.

horsepower: A unit for measuring the power of an engine.

stable: Firmly fixed and not likely to fail or give way.

wind pressure: The force that wind has on a structure.

winglets: Small structures that extend from motorcycle frames and help create downforce.

INDEX

TO LEARN MORE

Finding more information is as easy as 1, 2, 3.

1. Go to www.factsurfer.com
2. Enter "superfastmotorcycles" into the search box.
3. Choose your book to see a list of websites.